remember

LITTLE BIGHORN

remember

LITTLE BIGHORN

Indians, Soldiers, and Scouts Tell Their Stories

Paul Robert Walker

with a foreword by **John A. Doerner,**
Little Bighorn Battlefield National Monument

NATIONAL GEOGRAPHIC

WASHINGTON, D.C.

For those who died, those who survived, and those who still search for the truth.

Compilation copyright © 2006 Paul Robert Walker; reprinted in
paperback and library binding, 2015
Published by the National Geographic Society.
All rights reserved. Reproduction of the whole or any part of the
contents without written permission from the publisher is prohibited.

STAFF FOR THIS BOOK
Suzanne Patrick Fonda, *Project Editor*
David M. Seager, *Art Director*
Callie Broaddus, *Associate Designer*
Lori Epstein, *Senior Photo Editor*
Carl Mehler, *Director of Maps*
Thomas L. Gray, Joseph F. Ochlak, Michelle H. Picard, Tibor G. Tóth,
    Gregory Ugiansky, Paul Robert Walker, NG Maps, and
    The M Factory, *Map Research and Production*
Paige Towler, *Editorial Assistant*
Ruthie Thompson, *Production Designer*
Rebecca Hinds, *Managing Editor*
R. Gary Colbert, *Production Director*
Lewis R. Bassford, *Production Manager*
Jennifer Hoff, *Manager, Production Services*

PUBLISHED BY THE NATIONAL GEOGRAPHIC SOCIETY
Gary E. Knell, *President and CEO*
John M. Fahey, *Chairman of the Board*
Melina Gerosa Bellows, *Chief Education Officer*
Declan Moore, *Chief Media Officer*
Hector Sierra, *Senior Vice President and General Manager, Book Division*

SENIOR MANAGEMENT TEAM, KIDS PUBLISHING AND MEDIA
Nancy Laties Feresten, *Senior Vice President;* Jennifer Emmett, *Vice
President, Editorial Director, Kids Books;* Julie Vosburgh Agnone, *Vice
President, Editorial Operations;* Rachel Buchholz, *Editor and Vice Presi-
dent,* NG Kids *magazine;* Michelle Sullivan, *Vice President, Kids Digital;*
Eva Absher-Schantz, *Design Director;* Jay Sumner, *Photo Director;* Hannah
August, *Marketing Director;* R. Gary Colbert, *Production Director*

DIGITAL
Anne McCormack, *Director;* Laura Goertzel, Sara Zeglin, *Producers;* Jed
Winer, *Special Projects Assistant;* Emma Rigney, *Creative Producer;* Brian
Ford, *Video Producer;* Bianca Bowman, *Assistant Producer;* Natalie Jones,
Senior Product Manager

Text is set in ITC New Baskerville.

The National Geographic Society is one of the world's largest nonprofit scientific and educational organizations. Founded in 1888 to "increase and diffuse
geographic knowledge," the Society's mission is to inspire people to care
about the planet. It reaches more than 400 million people worldwide each
month through its official journal, *National Geographic,* and other magazines;
National Geographic Channel; television documentaries; music; radio; films;
books; DVDs; maps; exhibitions; live events; school publishing programs;
interactive media; and merchandise. National Geographic has funded more
than 10,000 scientific research, conservation, and exploration projects and
supports an education program promoting geographic literacy.

For more information, please visit nationalgeographic.com,
call 1-800-NGS LINE (647-5463), or write to the following address:

NATIONAL GEOGRAPHIC SOCIETY
1145 17th Street N.W.
Washington, D.C. 20036-4688 U.S.A.

Visit us online at nationalgeographic.com/books

For librarians and teachers: ngchildrensbooks.org

More for kids from National Geographic: kids.nationalgeographic.com

For information about special discounts for bulk purchases, please contact
National Geographic Books Special Sales: ngspecsales@ngs.org

**National Geographic supports K–12 educators with ELA Common Core
Resources. Visit natgeoed.org/commoncore for more information.**

Printed in China
15/RRDS/1

ACKNOWLEDGMENTS
Thanks to John Doerner for his expert advice throughout this project,
to Glen Swanson for generously sharing his vast photo collection, and
to Chip Watts for leading this tenderfoot on an all-day ride across the
battlefield. Thanks also to Joe Medicine Crow for telling me stories he
heard from his great-uncle, White Man Runs Him, and other participants; to Douglas War Eagle for sharing new insights discovered by
the Crazy Horse family; and to Ernie LaPointe, great-grandson of Sitting
Bull, for enlightening me on his family and the Lakota spiritual path.

The Library of Congress cataloged the 2006 edition as follows:
Walker, Paul Robert.
  Remember Little Bighorn : Indians, soldiers, and scouts tell their
stories / written by Paul Robert Walker ; foreword by John A.
Doerner.
    p. cm.
  Includes bibliographical references and index.
  ISBN 0-7922-5521-6 (hardcover)—ISBN 0-7922-5522-4 (lib. bdg.)
  1. Little Bighorn, Battle of the, Mont., 1876—Personal narratives—
Juvenile literature. 2. Cheyenne Indians—Wars, 1876—Personal
narratives—Juvenile literature. 3. Dakota Indians—Wars, 1876—
Personal narratives—Juvenile literature. I. National Geographic
Society (U.S.) II. Title.
  E83.876.W35 2006
  973.8′2--dc22

                                    2005030929

2015 paperback edition ISBN: 978-1-4263-2246-4
2015 reinforced library edition ISBN: 978-1-4263-2351-5

PHOTO CREDITS
ABHB = Reproduced from *A Pictographic History of the Oglala Sioux,* by Amos
Bad Heart Bull, text by Helen H. Blish, published by the University of Nebraska
Press, 1967; DPL WHC = Denver Public Library, Western History Collection;
GS = Glen Swanson Collection; GW = Gene Westerberg Collection; LBBNM =
Little Bighorn Battlefield National Monument; MP = Painting by Martin Pate,
Newman, GA., courtesy Southeast Archeological Center, National Park Service;
NA = National Archives; NAA = National Anthropological Archives, Smithsonian
Institution; SAA/AR = Smithsonian American Art Museum, Washington, D.C./Art
Resource, NY
Cover, The Reed Remington Graff Collection, Dallas; image courtesy Art Gallery,
Inc., Dallas; 4–5, photo by Bill Moeller; 8, photo by Paul Robert Walker; 10, NA
77-hq-264809; 11, LBBNM; 12, NA NWDNS-FF-2F-10; 13 (upper), SAA/AR; 13
(lower), DPL WHC X-31790; 14, GS; 15 (upper), American Museum of Natural
History; 15 (lower), LBBNM; 17, SAA/AR; 18, GW; 19 (upper), GS; 19 (lower),
LBBNM; 20, © James Hautman; 21, LBBNM; 22, NA NWDS-111-FF-82531; 23
(upper), GS; 23 (lower), NAA INV 00523800; 24 (upper), courtesy Stands in Timber
family; 24 (lower), LBBNM; 25, LBBNM; 26 (upper), DPL WHC X-31214; 26 (lower),
GS; 27 (upper), LBBNM; 27 (lower), NAA INV 00506100; 28, ABHB Plate 158; 29
(upper), courtesy U.S. Military Academy Library; 29 (lower), LBBNM; 30, LBBNM;
31, GS; 32, ABHB by permission of the University of Nebraska Press. Copyright
© 1967 by the University of Nebraska Press. Copyright © renewed 1995 by the
University of Nebraska Press. Plate 130; 33, GS; 34, ABHB Plate 146; 35 (upper),
NAA INV 08584500; 35 (lower), Custer Battle Flag, 1876, Museum Purchase
with funds from the Hon. Don M. Dickinson, Photograph © 1996, The Detroit
Institute of Arts; 36, LBBNM; 37, LBBNM; 38, From the original painting by Mort
Künstler, "Custer's Last Stand," © 1986, Mort Künstler, Inc.; 39 (upper), LBBNM;
39 (lower), GS; 40 (upper and middle), GS; 40 (lower), NAA Neg. 3179-B1; 41
(upper), MP; 41 (lower), GS; 42, NAA INV 08705700; 43 (upper), GS; 43 (lower),
NAA INV 06108700; 44 (upper), Rock Island Arsenal Museum; 44 (lower), GS; 45,
Amon Carter Museum, #1964.194, Otto Becker, after Cassilly Adams, "Custer's
Last Fight," chromolithograph 1896; 46, Courtesy of the Autrey National Center,
Southwest Museum, Los Angeles, #1026.G.1; 47 (left, center left), GS; 47 (center),
LBBNM; 47 (center right, right), GW; 48, National Geographic Society, painting
by Roy Andersen; 49 (both), GS; 50 (both), GS; 51 (upper), LBBNM; 51 (lower),
MP; 52 (upper), ABHB Plate #85; 52 (lower), NAA Neg. #3409-B; 53 (upper), GS;
53 (lower), LBBNM; 54, GS; 55, GS; 56, NAA Neg. 3194-C. All maps copyright ©
National Geographic Society.

*COVER: "Last Glow of a Passing Nation," by Richard Lorenz (1914) captures the
Indians' moment of triumph over Custer and members of the Seventh Cavalry as
other warriors ride off toward Reno Hill.*

TITLE PAGE: Custer Hill on a stormy summer day

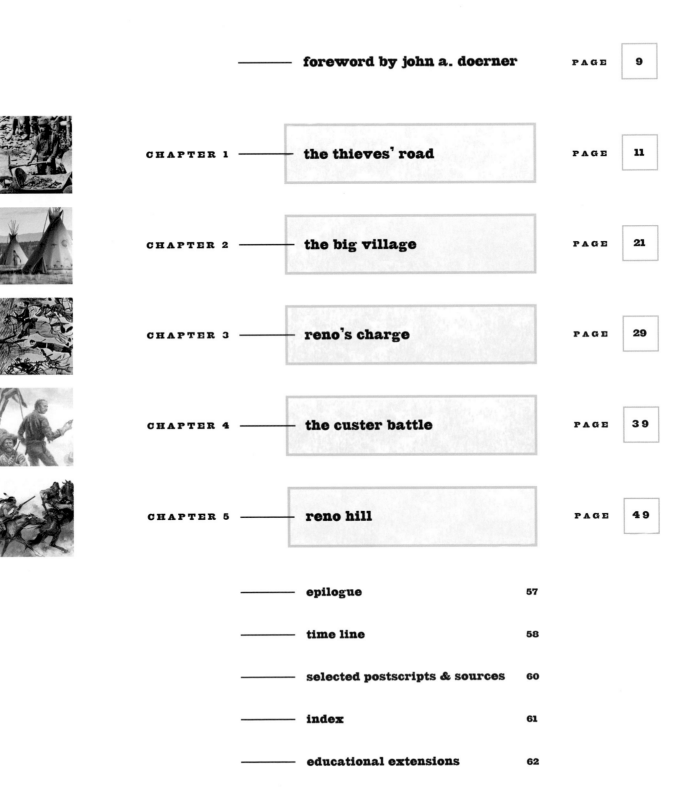

Chief Historian for Little Bighorn Battlefield National Monument
John Doerner gestures toward an interpretive sign in Deep Ravine, where
Crazy Horse led his charge from across the river and where the last of
Custer's men may have died.

Perhaps no other battle in American history captures the public's imagination more than the Battle of Little Bighorn. On June 25–26, 1876, two culturally opposite forces clashed along the Little Bighorn River in present-day southeastern Montana. One was fighting to open new land for settlement, the other to preserve a nomadic way of life. The battle is unquestionably the most dramatic and glorified ever fought on the Great Plains.

In what became known as Custer's Last Stand, 1,500 to 2,000 Lakota Sioux, Cheyenne, and Arapaho warriors—united under their political and spiritual leader *Tatanka-Iyotanka* (Sitting Bull), Hunkpapa Lakota—wiped out Lieutenant Colonel George Armstrong Custer and the 209 men of the Seventh Cavalry who were under his immediate command. Fifty-three others under the commands of Major Marcus A. Reno and Captain Frederick Benteen also were killed.

The "Custer Massacre" shocked a nation that was in the midst of celebrating the 100th anniversary of its Declaration of Independence from Great Britain. To the Lakota Sioux, Cheyenne, and Arapaho, however, this epic battle was their greatest victory against the United States Army in a long struggle to retain their homelands. Little Bighorn made Custer a national hero and became a rallying point for the U.S. military's retaliation against the Plains Indians. By 1877 most of the Lakota Sioux and Cheyenne had been forced onto reservations or had fled with Sitting Bull to Canada.

Today, Little Bighorn Battlefield National Monument is a special place, unlike any other battlefield in the world. Visitors see a powerful cultural landscape largely unchanged since the battle was fought in 1876. White marble headstones erected in 1890 by the War Department mark actual Seventh Cavalry casualty sites. Beginning in 1999, I led efforts for the National Park Service to erect red granite headstones throughout the battlefield to commemorate known Lakota and Cheyenne casualty sites, bringing a unique balance and perspective for park visitors. There are now 17 markers.

Paul Robert Walker brings the historic events and participants of the Battle of Little Bighorn into proper perspective through careful and exhaustive research. He has walked the hallowed ground at Little Bighorn Battlefield National Monument, knows the story well, and brings the history of that fateful battle to life.

The winds of change sound out along the Little Bighorn since those fateful days in June 1876. Many ceremonies have marked anniversaries of the battle. Veterans from both sides returned to the battlefield on many occasions to recount brave war deeds, shake hands with former enemies, and bury the hatchet in peace and friendship. They are but memories now, faded into history, but their legacy lives on as descendants are joined in common bond to this special place—to pay homage in their own unique way to a battle fought long ago along the Little Bighorn River.

John A. Doerner
John A. Doerner

Custer's Black Hills expedition enters Castle Creek Valley on July 26, 1874. For Custer and his soldiers, the expedition was like a summer vacation, with hunting, parties, concerts, and baseball games. To the Lakota Sioux it was a serious invasion of their sacred territory.

the thieves' road

In the summer of 1874, Lieutenant Colonel George Armstrong Custer led a long, snaking line of 1,000 soldiers, 100 Indian scouts, a 16-piece band, and 110 supply wagons into the Black Hills of what is now South Dakota.

The Sioux Indians considered this expedition to be a violation of a treaty they had signed six years earlier with the United States government, which promised a vast reservation, including the Hills, where they could live free of white interference. The Sioux called Custer's trail "The Thieves' Road," but they did not resist the soldiers at this time; they watched and waited to see what would happen.

Custer had been ordered to find a good site for a fort on the western side of the hills, to find a connection to a known route from Fort Laramie to the southwest, and to explore the beautiful land that few whites had seen—an enchanting world of thick pine forests and grassy meadows, clear springs and lakes, jagged rock formations, and abundant wildlife. In one report, Custer wrote, "No portion of the United States can boast of a richer or better pasturage, purer water, . . . and of greater advantages generally to the farmer or stock raiser."

It would be a wonderful place for farming or ranching, but that was not the news that set America on fire. The real excitement began when some of Custer's men found small bits of gold. Before he left the Hills, Custer sent a scout to carry reports to frontier newspapers. Then, on his way back to Fort Abraham Lincoln in present-day North Dakota, he wrote the words that would lead to death for Custer and hundreds of his men: "The miners report that they found gold among the roots of the grass. . . . It has not required an expert to find gold in the Black Hills, and men without former experience in mining have discovered it at an expense of but little time and labor."

By the time Custer returned to Fort Abraham Lincoln, the northern frontier was buzzing with excitement over a new gold rush. America was in the middle of an economic depression, and many men were out of work.

Lieutenant Colonel George Armstrong Custer

A gold mining crew working in Deadwood, Dakota Territory, in 1876. By the time of the Battle of Little Bighorn, Deadwood was already a thriving town with thousands of miners working on land that had been promised to the Sioux.

Soon, hundreds of miners streamed into the Black Hills, hoping to make their fortunes. At first the army tried to keep them out; they burned the wagons and supplies of those who entered the Hills and escorted the intruders off the reservation. But the miners kept on coming.

Faced with a growing gold rush on Indian land, the U.S. government tried to buy the Black Hills. In late September 1875, more than 10,000 Sioux, Cheyenne, and Arapaho gathered in northern Nebraska to meet with government representatives. These were mostly "agency Indians," who lived on the Great Sioux Reservation and accepted food and supplies from government agencies just outside the reservation boundaries. But there were also several hundred warriors from "hunting bands" who refused to accept government handouts and ignored the reservation boundaries, as they continued their traditional life, following the buffalo across the northern plains.

The buffalo was the main source of food, clothing, and shelter for the Plains Indians. As whites built railroads through the West and white hunters slaughtered the animals for their hides, the great herds grew smaller and smaller. In 1832–33, when George Catlin painted this scene, there were some 30 million buffalo west of the Mississippi. By 1889, there were fewer than a thousand.

The most powerful leaders of the hunting bands were Sitting Bull and Crazy Horse, who never signed treaties with the whites and wanted only to be left alone. Sitting Bull and Crazy Horse refused to attend the conference, but one of Crazy Horse's warriors, Little Big Man, made their point loud and clear. Riding into the conference, stripped and painted for battle, he brandished his rifle in the air and shouted, "I will kill the first chief who speaks for selling the Black Hills!"

Despite this threat, some reservation leaders were willing to sell the Hills if the price was high enough to support their people. But the government offer was too low, and the conference ended in failure.

A month later, in early November, President Ulysses S. Grant held a private meeting at the White House. Although he had first gained fame as a tough, hard-fighting general in the Civil War, Grant had tried to treat the Indians fairly with a plan called the Peace Policy. Now he decided to go back to the policy he knew best: War.

At this meeting, Grant and his advisors made two important decisions. First, although white miners in the Black Hills would still be considered "illegal," the army would no longer enforce the law. Second, all Sioux living off the reservation, including the followers of Sitting Bull and Crazy Horse, would be given until

Little Big Man

13

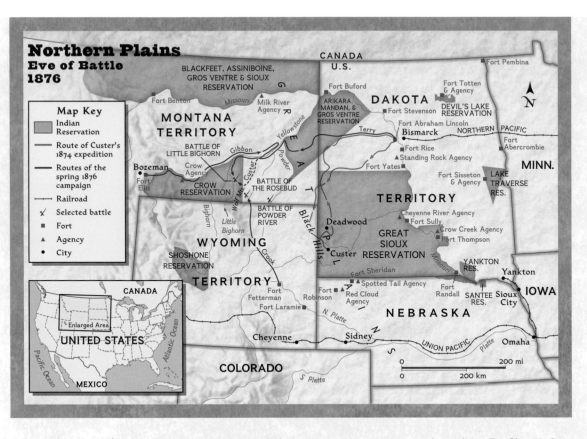

Northern Plains
Eve of Battle 1876

Map Key
- ▨ Indian Reservation
- — Route of Custer's 1874 expedition
- — Routes of the spring 1876 campaign
- ⊢⊢ Railroad
- ⤬ Selected battle
- ■ Fort
- ▲ Agency
- ● City

By 1876, four large reservations and several smaller ones had been established in the Dakota and Montana Territories, with a network of forts and agencies around them. The discovery of gold in the Black Hills in 1874—and, later, pressure from farmers and ranchers—led the government to greatly reduce the size of most reservations.

General George Crook

January 31, 1876, to report to one of the government agencies. Any Indian who did not report would be considered "hostile" and be hunted down by the army.

That December, runners were sent out from the agencies to inform the hunting bands of the President's order. In the harsh winter of the northern Plains, it was difficult to even find the bands. And to men like Sitting Bull and Crazy Horse, the idea of leading their people on a dangerous journey through the snow seemed ridiculous. Winter was a quiet time of camping in a place protected from the cold winds, surviving on dried buffalo meat, and staying warm under buffalo robes beside a fire. If there was anything to discuss with the whites, they would do it in the spring—if they did it at all.

Grant and his advisors knew this, so it seems likely that they set the deadline in the middle of winter as a way to force a war. Sure enough, not a single Indian reported to the agencies by January 31. The next day, the Secretary of the Interior—who had responsibility for the Indians under the Peace Policy—wrote to the Secretary of War that "the said Indians are hereby turned over to the War Department for such action on the part of the army as you deem proper under the circumstances."

A month later, General George Crook left a fort in Wyoming with 900 soldiers and headed north into the hunting grounds of eastern Montana. Crook was one of the most experienced Indian-fighting officers in the army, but he was not prepared for the harsh northern winter, and his men struggled through the snow. On the morning of March 17, a force under Crook's second-in-command, Colonel Joseph J. Reynolds, attacked a small village of Cheyenne and some Sioux on the Powder River. An 18-year-old Cheyenne warrior named Wooden Leg later recalled the terror caused by the charging soldiers: "Women screamed. Children cried for their mothers. Old people tottered and hobbled away to get out of reach of the bullets singing among the lodges. Braves seized whatever weapons they had and tried to meet the attack. I owned a muzzle-loading rifle, but I had no bullets for it. I owned also a cap-and-ball six shooter, but I had loaned it to Star, a cousin. . . . In turn, he had let me have bow and arrows."

Despite the surprise attack and superiority of the soldier's weapons, the warriors bravely protected their families as they fled from the village. Only two Indians were killed, one Cheyenne and one Sioux. The soldiers stole the precious pony herd, but that night the warriors stole the ponies back.

Wooden Leg

This drawing by Wooden Leg shows him rescuing two children during the attack on the Cheyenne village along the Powder River. "The girl behind me clasped her arms about my waist," he recalled. "I wrapped an arm about the boy in front of me. With my free arm and hand I guided my horse the best I could. . . . I got the two children out of danger. Then I went back to help in the fight."

The greatest loss came when the soldiers burned the entire village and all the possessions the Indians had left behind. Now they had nothing but their weapons, their horses, and the clothes on their backs.

Cold and hungry, the Cheyenne joined the village of Crazy Horse, who welcomed them and gave them what he could. Crazy Horse's people were poor that winter, so he led the two villages together to the large camp of Sitting Bull, the most powerful leader among the western Sioux—or Lakota—who did not live on the reservation. Sitting Bull's people were rich, not in money, but in all they needed to live, and they welcomed the Cheyenne in an impressive display of generosity that Wooden Leg remembered well: "They flooded us with gifts of everything needful. Crowds of their men and women were going among us to find out and to supply our wants. . . . Oh what good hearts they had! I never can forget the generosity of Sitting Bull's Uncpapa Sioux* on that day."

Now the three villages traveled together, moving up and down the rivers and streams that cut through the great buffalo range of northern Wyoming and eastern Montana. The same treaty that had created the Great Sioux Reservation also gave the Indians the right to hunt in this area, but with the President's order and the attack on the Cheyenne village, they knew that soldiers were hunting them, just as Indians hunted the buffalo.

As the large village continued to move that spring, they were joined by other bands of Lakota, Cheyenne, and eastern Sioux. By early June, there were perhaps 400 lodges and about 3,000 people, including 800 warriors. It was a good time for the Indians, following the buffalo, feasting, visiting, and preparing robes for trade.

In a camp on Rosebud Creek, Sitting Bull held a sun dance, the great religious ceremony of the Plains Indians. Before the dance, he offered a "scarlet blanket"—blood from one hundred pieces of flesh cut from his arms—to *Wakan Tanka,* the Great Mysterious, the Lakota name for God. Then he danced for hours around a tall pole cut from a cottonwood tree, fasting and gazing at the sun. Finally, he stopped and stared into the sky at a vision of

• The modern spelling of this tribal name is Hunkpapa.

soldiers and horses falling upside down, as thick as grasshoppers, and dropping into an Indian village. "These soldiers do not possess ears," a voice proclaimed. "They are to die, but you are not supposed to take their spoils."

By this time, Indian scouts had reported two groups of soldiers, one approaching from the south, the other from the west along the Yellowstone River. The soldiers from the south were General Crook's command, returning to the field with 1,000 soldiers and more than 260 Crow and Shoshone scouts, traditional enemies of the Sioux. The soldiers from the west were 450 men under Colonel John Gibbon, with a small group of Crow. Though the Indians didn't know it, there was also a large column marching from the east: 925 soldiers and about 40 Arikara scouts under General Alfred Terry. Most of this column was the Seventh Cavalry commanded by Custer, the same soldiers whose expedition into the Black Hills had started the trouble in the first place.

After the sun dance, the village moved on over a low, rugged range called

The sun dance was the great religious ritual of the Plains Indians. As shown in this 1835–37 painting by George Catlin, the dancers often suspended themselves from the central pole with a strip of buffalo hide tied through their chest skin. Sitting Bull made a different offering: 100 small pieces of flesh cut from his arms.

the Wolf Mountains and followed a small creek toward a larger stream they called the Greasy Grass—known to whites as the Little Bighorn. Even before the Indians made camp, scouts reported that the Rosebud Valley behind them was "black with soldiers." Though the chiefs discouraged attack, the young warriors were so excited to battle the soldiers that their leaders decided to join them. Some 500 warriors rode through the night, led by Crazy Horse and Sitting Bull, who was still weak from the sun dance but accompanied them to offer inspiration.

Early on the morning of June 17, 1876, the warriors approached Crook's army of about 1,300 men, including Crow and Shoshone scouts. It was the scouts who saved the soldiers, holding off the Sioux and Cheyenne long enough to allow the surprised "bluecoats" to prepare themselves. The battle raged back and forth throughout the day, up and down the long valley in a confusion of men and horses and guns. "It was a great fight," recalled a Cheyenne leader named Two Moons, "much smoke and dust."

George Custer (center, standing with arms folded and in buckskin jacket) and his wife, Libby (seated to his right with small black hat) pose with friends and family during a picnic on the Little Heart River, near Fort Abraham Lincoln, in 1875. Including George Custer, ten of the men in this photo would fight at the Little Bighorn; only two would survive.

The Indians fought with a new power and confidence that amazed the whites. "They were in front, rear, flanks, and on every hilltop, far and near," a soldier later reported. "I had been in several Indian battles, but never saw so many Indians at one time before, . . . or so brave."

General Crook claimed victory when the warriors rode away that afternoon, but the real victory belonged to the Indians. Crook was so disturbed by the force of the attack that he retreated to his base camp in northern Wyoming and spent the next weeks building fortifications to protect his soldiers. This removed Crook's large army from the field, just as the soldiers under Gibbon, Terry, and Custer prepared for an attack of their own.

As his people mourned their dead and prepared to move on, Sitting Bull knew that another battle was coming. The Battle of the Rosebud had been fought in the camp of the soldiers. His vision had been clear: The soldiers would die coming into an Indian village.

Two Moons

This artwork by Wooden Leg shows his rescue of Black Sun, a wounded Cheyenne warrior, at the Battle of the Rosebud. "All of his body was colored yellow," recalled Wooden Leg. "On his head he wore the stuffed skin of a weasel." Despite this protective "medicine," Black Sun died of his wounds that night. The curved lines at the bottom represent the tracks of horses.

Lakota people go about daily chores in a peaceful village—much like the great village on the Little Bighorn—in this modern painting by James Hautman.

the big village

On the morning after the battle, the Indian village moved farther down the creek and up the valley of the Greasy Grass, or Little Bighorn. They camped for six nights on the eastern bank, near a large herd of buffalo. Here they held victory dances for the Battle of the Rosebud, for they did not celebrate in the same camp where they mourned their dead.

It was here, too, that many bands began to arrive from the agencies. Some people left the agencies every summer to hunt and participate in traditional ceremonies, but the 1876 migration was larger than ever. Word had spread that Sitting Bull was leading a strong, powerful village that would fight for the Black Hills and the right to live as hunters.

In less than a week, the village more than doubled in size, until there were about 1,000 lodges, or tepees, housing 7,000 people, with some 1,800 warriors. They camped in 6 large circles, each with its own leaders, heralds, and shamans. One circle was made up of Northern Cheyenne, with some Southern Cheyenne and Arapaho visitors. The other circles were different groups or "subtribes" of Lakota. Sitting Bull's people, the Hunkpapa, were the largest, joined by some eastern Sioux. There were also large circles of Oglala, Miniconjou, and Sans Arc, and a circle combining people from the Blackfeet, Brulé, and Two Kettle subtribes. A Cheyenne named Antelope Woman remembered, "There were more Indians in those six camps than I ever saw together anywhere else."

While camping in this place, scouts reported antelope herds to the north, near the junction of what we call the Bighorn and Little Bighorn Rivers. So the chiefs decided to head back down the Greasy Grass for an antelope hunt.

The moving village was an amazing sight: 7,000 people, 10,000 horses or more, and hundreds of dogs, carrying all their belongings on the horses' backs or in travois, a wooden frame pulled by a horse or dog. "Our trail . . . that summer could have been followed by a blind person," said Wooden Leg.

Antelope Woman

This drawing of an Indian village on the move, by Charles M. Russell (1905), shows the carrying system used by the Lakota, Cheyenne, and other tribes. Called a travois, it consisted of two long poles tied together across a horse's back. Belongings and food were lashed securely to the poles, which trailed behind the horse. Dogs sometimes pulled smaller travois.

By the afternoon of Saturday, June 24, the people were again settled in their six camp circles, spread for a mile or so along the western bank of the Greasy Grass. The little stream, about five feet deep, cold from the melting winter snow, wound its way through banks of cottonwood trees beneath towering bluffs on the eastern side, across from the village. Beyond the bluffs were tilted, rolling hills cut with dry creek beds and ravines. To the west, away from the river and the village, were wider, flat hills or "benchlands" where the Indian pony herd grazed.

That evening, just before sunset, Sitting Bull stripped to his breech cloth, put on ceremonial paint, and loosened his long hair from its braids. He gathered offerings of a sacred pipe, tobacco, and a buffalo robe and set off with his nephew One Bull, a young warrior who had recently married and lived in a tepee near his uncle's. The two men crossed the river at a shallow spot and climbed through an opening in the bluffs, up into the rolling hills. There on the crest of a ridge that gave him a view of the surrounding land, Sitting Bull presented his offerings to Wakan Tanka and prayed for his people: "Wakan Tanka, pity me. In the name of the nation I offer You this pipe. Wherever the

Sun, Moon, Earth, Four Winds, there You are always. Father, save the people, I beg You. We wish to live! Guard us against all misfortunes and calamities. Take pity!"

Although Sitting Bull was worried, his people were happy that evening, enjoying the warm summer night and the pleasure of visiting and feasting with relatives and friends.

"That night we had a dance," Wooden Leg remembered, "a social affair for young people, not a ceremonial or war dance." There were dances in the Sioux camps as well, and when a friend suggested they "go and dance awhile with the Sioux girls," Wooden Leg, his friend, and two other young Cheyenne went over to the neighboring camp of the Sans Arc Lakota.

Sitting Bull

"Pretty soon the girls were asking us to dance," he recalled—it was the custom for the girls to do the asking. "The Sioux women gave us plenty of food. We were treated well, so we did not go elsewhere nor back to our own people. We stayed there and danced throughout the remainder of that night."

While most of the dancing was for fun, some recalled a different kind of dance that night, the Dying Dance. According to Cheyenne historian John Stands in Timber, who heard the story from warriors who were there, a group of Lakota boys took a suicide vow that night, which meant that they would fight until the death in the next battle. A few Cheyenne boys also took the vow, and the Lakota held a dance for all of them in one of their camps. "When those boys came in they could not hear themselves talk," Stands in Timber wrote, "there was so much noise, with the crowd packed around and both the men and women singing."

One Bull

The dancing ended at dawn, and there was a great parade for the suicide boys, with the boys walking in front and an old man on either side "announcing to the public to look at these boys well; they would never come back after the next battle." Many other dancers just went home to sleep. Wooden Leg was so exhausted that he did not go into his family's lodge, but "dropped down on the ground behind it." Others slept in their tepees or under cottonwood trees, getting as much rest as they could before the heat of the summer day.

John Stands in Timber

Lieutenant Charles Varnum

At this exact moment, in the first clear light of dawn, a small group of Crow scouts serving with Custer's Seventh Cavalry gazed down upon the village from a ridge about 15 miles away—the same ridge that the Lakota and Cheyenne had crossed as they moved from the Rosebud to the Little Bighorn. Although the distance was great, and the village itself was hidden behind another ridge, the trained eyes of the Crow recognized the smoke of early morning campfires and the vast pony herd on the benchland. It was a big village, they agreed, perhaps the biggest they had ever seen.

Lieutenant Charles Varnum, in command of the scouts, remembered that the Crow handed him a cheap telescope and told him to look for the smoke and "worms crawling on the grass," which would be the pony herd. Varnum had excellent eyes, but he was tired from being up most of the night, and he could see neither smoke nor worms. Still, he believed the Crow—it was their country, and they knew what to look for. So he sent a note back to Custer, who was then camping eight miles behind them.

After sending the note, Varnum noticed two Indians about a mile away. He tried to head them off, but they changed direction. Later that morning, he saw a group of six or seven Indians, riding along the crest of a ridge, moving in the direction of Custer's command. "The crest where we were was higher than they were," he remembered, "and as they rode along the crest, reflected against the sky, their ponies looked as big as elephants." The Indians quickly disappeared, but Varnum was convinced they had seen the dust of the cavalry, now approaching the Crow's Nest in response to Varnum's note.

The lieutenant met Custer and guided him up to look for himself, crouching on the ground and gazing though the same cheap telescope. The light was brighter now, with a glare from the morning sun, and it was even more difficult to see into the distance. "I've got about as good eyes as anybody," Custer muttered in disgust, "and I can't see any village, Indians, or anything else."

Custer's chief of scouts, Mitch Boyer—born of a French father and Sioux mother—had been with Varnum and the Crow earlier that morning, and he, too, had seen the signs. "Well, General," he said, "if you don't find more

Four of the six Crow scouts who led the Seventh Cavalry to the Little Bighorn are shown here, visiting the battlefield in 1908: (left to right) White Man Runs Him, Hairy Moccasin, Curly, and Goes Ahead. The Crow volunteered to scout for the army to protect their traditional lands from the Sioux. The Battle of Little Bighorn took place on the Crow Reservation.

Indians in that valley than you ever saw together, you can hang me." Although Custer was only a Lieutenant Colonel, Boyer and the other men called him "General" because he had earned an honorary general's rank in the Civil War.

Custer sprang to his feet and snarled, "It would do a damned sight of good to hang you, wouldn't it?" Varnum remembered this clearly, because Custer seldom swore; he was angry and wanted to see the village for himself. Riding back to his troops, now camped about a mile behind, he borrowed an expensive set of binoculars from one of his officers and returned to the ridge. This time he saw some "cloud-like objects" that the scouts said were pony herds.

By the time Custer returned again to his main camp, a group of soldiers reported that they had discovered several Indians trying to open a wooden box of a hard bread called hardtack that had fallen from one of the mules during the night. This was bad news. Varnum and the scouts had told him of the Indians they had seen, and he was now not only convinced that he had found the Indian camp but also that the camp had found him.

Custer's original plan was to hide his men all day, to rest from their ride the night before, and then to ride again under the cover of darkness to attack the village at dawn. This tactic had worked for him before, and it would allow time for another large force under Custer's commanding officer, General Alfred

Mitch Boyer

These field glasses belonged to Captain Frederick Benteen and were used at the Battle of Little Bighorn. The expensive glasses that Custer borrowed on the morning of June 25 were lost with Custer.

Terry, to reach the junction of the Bighorn and Little Bighorn Rivers, where they could capture any Indians who tried to escape. It was a good plan, but now that his men had been discovered, Custer feared that the Indians would run away and disappear into the Plains. So he decided to attack then and there, in broad daylight, without support from General Terry.

Custer has been criticized for this decision—some have called him insane–but it was not that unreasonable considering his previous experience with Indian warfare and his pride in the Seventh Cavalry. Based on the campsites his scouts had examined along the trail and reports from the War Department about Indians leaving the agencies, he guessed there might be no more than 1,500 warriors. That was not far from the truth, but Custer did not know about the Battle of the Rosebud and the new, united confidence of the Indians. According to one of his officers, three nights before the battle, Custer had said that his Seventh Cavalry, with 647 men, including some civilians and the Indian scouts, "could whip any force that would be able to combine against him, [and] that if the regiment could not, no other regiment in the service could." This was arrogant, but it was not crazy.

As Custer's army prepared for the attack, the people in the great village enjoyed a warm, lazy summer morning. Some were out with their horses, watching them graze or leading them to water. Others picked wild turnips. But many of them, especially, the young people, went swimming in the cool clear water of the Greasy Grass.

Wooden Leg woke exhausted and went into the family tepee where his mother made breakfast for him and told him to go take a bath in the river. "My brother Yellow Hair and I went together. Other Indians, of all ages and both sexes, were splashing in the waters of the river. The sun was high, the weather was hot. The cool water felt good to my skin. When my brother and I had dabbled there a few minutes we came

Here, on the 1874 Black Hills expedition, Custer (seated) poses with Arikara scouts (left to right) Bloody Knife, Goose, and Little Sioux. All three fought with Major Reno at Little Bighorn, where Bloody Knife was killed and Goose was wounded. The soldier is Private John Burkman, who took care of Custer's horses. According to him, Tuck and Bleuch, the dogs shown here, stayed with the pack train during the battle.

out and sought the shelter of some shade trees. We sat there a little while, talking of the good times each of us had enjoyed during the previous night. We sprawled out to lie down and talk. Before we knew it, both of us were sound asleep."

Antelope Woman went with another young lady to visit friends among the Miniconjou, near the other end of the great village from the Cheyenne camp. "We found our women friends bathing in the river, and we joined them," she remembered. "Other groups, men, women, and children were playing in the water at many places along the stream. Some boys were fishing. All of us were having a good time. . . . Nobody was thinking of any battle coming."

A young Oglala boy named Black Elk—not quite 13 years old—couldn't decide if he wanted to swim or not. He had been up at dawn to care for his family's horses, and by the time he got back to the village and ate breakfast, he began to feel strange. For Black Elk strange feelings had meaning. At the age of nine, he had been blessed with a great vision, and ever since that time, he could often feel when things were about to happen. "I did not feel right," he later said. "I had a funny feeling all this time, because I thought that in an hour or so something terrible might happen."

Black Elk

Reno's men, pursued by Lakota and Cheyenne warriors, plunge into the Little Bighorn River in this drawing by Lakota artist Amos Bad Heart Bull. He was seven years old when he witnessed the battle and learned about its details from his father and uncles.

reno's charge

The sun was hot and high in the sky when the regiment halted just across the divide between the Rosebud and Little Bighorn valleys. It was seven minutes past noon, Chicago time—the official time of the regiment—but it was still late morning by the local sun time of eastern Montana, the only time the Indians knew.

Here Custer organized his 12 companies of soldiers into 4 groups. He kept 5 companies under his own command and assigned 3 each to his senior officers, Major Marcus Reno and Captain Frederick Benteen. While Custer and Reno followed a dry creek down to the Little Bighorn, Benteen swept out to the left, across a series of ridges to catch any Indians trying to escape and to get a better view of the valley. The 12th company, under Captain Thomas McDougall, accompanied the slow-moving mule train carrying food, supplies, and extra ammunition.

Major Marcus Reno

After two hours of riding along the creek, the men under Custer and Reno reached a single tepee with a dead warrior inside on a burial scaffold, one of the Lakotas who had been killed at the Battle of the Rosebud. The scouts had arrived before the main troops, and from a knoll they were able to get their first clear view of the Little Bighorn valley. A white civilian scout, George Herendeen, recalled that they saw "a heavy cloud of dust and some stock [horses], apparently running. We could see beyond the stream a few Indians on the hills, riding very fast, seemingly running away."

When this news was relayed to Custer, he ordered Major Reno to take the Arikara scouts and trot ahead with his troops. About 30 minutes later, after new sightings of Indians who appeared to be running away, Custer ordered Reno to "charge the village . . . and you will be supported by the whole outfit." Reno now had about 175 men in all, while Custer had about 225, including some scouts and civilians. Benteen and McDougall, with almost 250 men between them, still lagged far behind.

George Herendeen

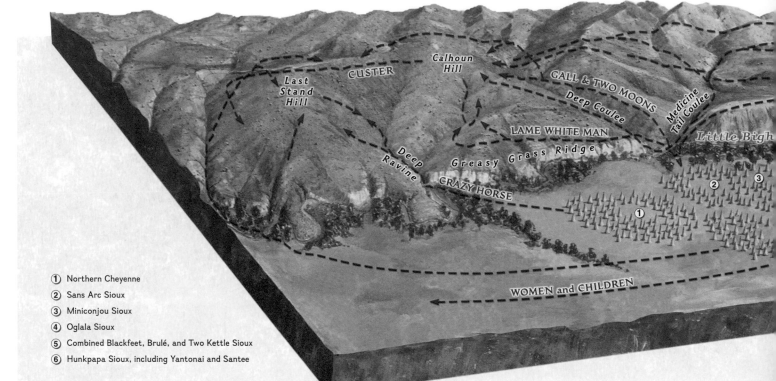

Little Bigh

① Northern Cheyenne
② Sans Arc Sioux
③ Miniconjou Sioux
④ Oglala Sioux
⑤ Combined Blackfeet, Brulé, and Two Kettle Sioux
⑥ Hunkpapa Sioux, including Yantonai and Santee

Private William O. Taylor

Major Reno turned off the trail and headed for the village, thinking Custer and his troops would follow. Crossing the Little Bighorn at a natural ford, he paused to let his horses and men drink. Private William O. Taylor remembered that the river was "some fifty to seventy feet wide . . . two to four feet deep of clear, icy cold water. Into it our horses plunged without any urging, their thirst was great and also their riders. While waiting for them to drink I took off my hat and, shaping the brim into a scoop, leaned over, filled it and drank the last drop of water I was to have for over twenty-four long hours."

As he forded the river, George Herendeen heard one Crow scout shout to another, "The Sioux are coming out to meet us." Herendeen understood the Crow language, so he told Major Reno, who immediately sent a messenger back to Custer, telling him that the Indians were not running away at all—they were strong and coming out to fight.

With the Arikara scouts fanning out to the left to run off the Sioux pony herd, Reno's troops rode toward the village, first at a fast walk, then a trot. During this approach, several men reported seeing Custer up on the bluffs on the other side of the river. Private Henry Petring remembered, "I saw Custer over across the river on the bluffs, waving his hat. Some of the men said: 'There goes Custer. He is up to something, for he is waving

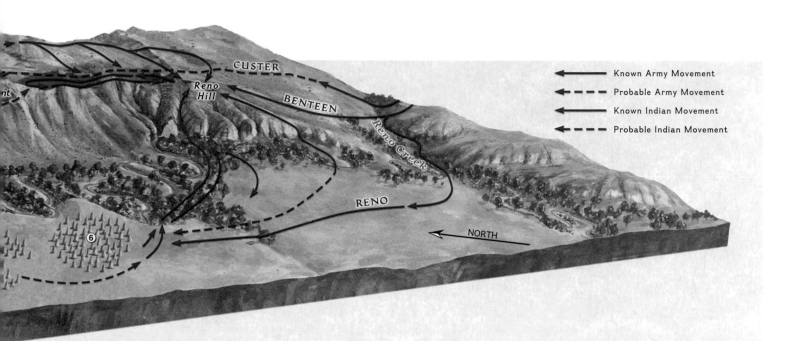

his hat.'" They soon had more immediate concerns than Custer.

"As we came nearer," Private Taylor recalled, "[we] could distinguish mounted men riding in every direction, some in circles, others passing back and forth. . . . Then as little puffs of smoke were seen and the 'Ping' of bullets spoke out plainly, we were ordered to charge."

Now Reno's soldiers rode full speed toward the Indian defenders. At first, it seemed easy—too easy—as Reno described in his official report: "I deployed and . . . charged down the valley, driving the Indians with great ease for about 2½ miles. I however soon saw that I was being drawn into some trap . . . I could not see Custer or any other support and at the same time the very earth seemed to grow Indians and they were running toward me in swarms and from all directions."

Some of Reno's men got close enough to fire into the Hunkpapa village. While most of the bullets flew too high, clipping the tops of the tepees, a few hit their marks, including a barrage that killed the two wives and three children of the Hunkpapa war chief, Gall. "It made my heart bad," he said. "After that I killed all my enemies with the hatchet."

Faced with perhaps 150 Indian warriors, with hundreds more on the way, Reno ordered his men to dismount and form a skirmish line. Every fourth man stayed on his own horse and took the reins of three others, leading them to the safety of a thick grove of trees along the river. Private Taylor was a fourth man, and though he "wanted to be in the fight" he led a group of horses to the woods.

This map reflects the latest thinking on the location and extent of the Indian village along the western bank of the Little Bighorn River. It also shows the movements of Custer, Reno, Benteen, and Weir as well as Gall, Two Moons, Lame White Man, and Crazy Horse, who led the Indian counterattacks on June 25, 1876.

Gall

Despite Custer's fears of being discovered that morning, most Indian accounts suggest that they were surprised by the attack. They knew that soldiers were looking for them but did not expect a battle on that hot and lazy Sunday. Many remembered a Lakota boy named Deeds who went out with his father to look for stray horses. The two encountered the attackers on the other side of the river—probably Arikara scouts riding ahead of the soldiers—and one of them killed Deeds while his father escaped to warn the village.

Among the first to hear the warning was Sitting Bull's nephew One Bull, who lived near his uncle at the southern end of the Hunkpapa circle, the closest point in the village to Reno's line of attack: "I was a strong young man 22 years old. On the day of the fight I was sitting in my tepee combing my hair. . . . I saw a man named Fat Bear come running into camp and he said soldiers

Amos Bad Heart Bull portrays Crazy Horse (left) and Sitting Bull (right) inspiring their warriors to fight bravely against the soldiers invading their village. In truth, Sitting Bull and Crazy Horse were at opposite ends of the village when Reno attacked, but the spirit of the drawing captures the importance of these two great leaders.

were coming on the other side of the river and had killed a boy named Deeds. . . . Then I came out of my tepee and saw soldiers running their horses to our camp on [the] same side of the river. We could hear lots of shooting. I went to [the] tepee of my uncle, Sitting Bull, and said I was going to take part in the battle."

One Bull had an old muzzle-loading rifle, but Sitting Bull took the gun from his nephew's hands and handed him a traditional stone war club and his own sacred shield, made of rawhide and beautifully painted. "You will take my place," he said, "and go out and meet the soldiers. Parley [talk] with them, if you can. If they are willing, tell them I will talk peace with them."

One Bull's older brother, White Bull, was out with his horses when he heard the alarm and raced back through the camps, stopping to make sure his own family was safe before heading to his uncle's tepee. "When I got to Sitting Bull's camp," he remembered, "his wife, child and everyone ran away, and every man who could fight got on a horse and stood [his] ground."

Sitting Bull mounted his own horse, carrying a .44 caliber Winchester rifle and a .45 caliber pistol. "Brave up, boys!" he shouted. "It will be a hard time. Brave up!" Sitting Bull had been a great warrior in his youth, but now, in his early 40s, his role was to inspire the warriors while protecting the women and children.

Antelope Woman, still swimming near the Miniconjou circle, just beyond the Hunkpapa camp, remembered that two Lakota boys came running toward them, shouting "Soldiers are coming!"

"We heard shooting. We hid in the brush. The sounds of the shooting multiplied—pop—pop—pop—pop! We heard women and children screaming. Old men were calling the young warriors to battle. Young men were singing their war songs as they responded to the call. We peeped out. Throngs of Sioux men on horses were racing toward the skirt of timber, just south of the Uncpapa camp circle, where the guns were clattering. The horsemen warriors were dodging through a mass of women, children, and old people hurrying afoot to the benchland hills west of the camps."

Out on the front line, One Bull could see that it was too late for talking. In the spirit of his uncle, he took a moment to pray: "Have mercy on me

White Bull

Wakan Tanka, that I may have no sin." Then he raised his shield in the air and ordered the warriors to charge. But no one responded. White Bull, with another group of warriors, noticed that the soldiers had planted a flag in the ground to mark their position. "Whoever is a brave man will go get that flag," he shouted. But no one took this challenge, either.

For about ten minutes, the soldiers and Indians shot at each other at long range, while a group of Hunkpapa drove off the Arikara scouts who were trying to steal the horses, and then circled around the left side of the skirmish line. At about the same time, One Bull lifted Sitting Bull's shield again and led a charge toward the center of the line, riding low behind his pony with four other warriors behind him. Although One Bull was untouched by the soldiers' bullets, three warriors were killed and a fourth, Good Bear Boy, was wounded and fell to

This drawing by Amos Bad Heart Bull shows Crazy Horse leading his warriors against Reno. There are no known, authentic photos of Crazy Horse, but this art portrays him as he probably appeared that day, with hail spots painted on his body.

the ground. One Bull carried him back to safety in the Hunkpapa camp, while the soldiers retreated to a second skirmish line in front of the woods.

Further to the north, in the Oglala camp, Black Elk had overcome his "funny feeling" and decided to go swimming anyway. He put bear grease on his body and was on his way to the river when he heard the alarm from the Hunkpapa circle: "They are charging, the chargers are coming!" Black Elk was too young to fight, but his older brother had ridden off so quickly that he forgot his gun. So Black Elk's father told him to bring the gun to his brother. "I got on my horse and as I went I could see the dust flying . . . When the dust parted, I could see the soldiers. These men looked big and husky and tall."

Black Elk found his brother and gave him his gun. His brother told him to go home, but he had a six-shooter that had been given to him by his sister, so he decided to stay. "When I got to the timber," Black Elk recalled, "the soldiers were shooting above us and you could see the leaves falling down off the trees where the bullets struck."

Black Elk and others made a break for it, riding across a stretch of flat, open ground. "The soldiers began to shoot at us," he remembered, "and all we heard was: 'Take courage, don't be like a woman.' Some of them said: 'Take courage, the helpless are out of their breath.'" And then the battle turned with the arrival of Black Elk's cousin Crazy Horse, leading Cheyenne, Miniconjou, and Oglala warriors from the far end of the village.

"Close after the crying about courage," said Black Elk, "we heard that Crazy Horse was coming. He was riding a white-faced horse. Everyone hollered: 'Crazy Horse is coming!' Just then I heard the bunch [of women, children, and older men] on the hillside to the west crying: *"Hokahey!"* and making the tremolo. We heard also the eagle bone whistles. . . . I could hear the thunder of the ponies charging."

Around the time that Crazy Horse arrived, Reno ordered his men to retreat into the timber. By this point in the battle, only two or three soldiers had been killed. But now, with the reinforcements led by Crazy Horse, the Indians circled the timber and drew closer and closer with their fire, some entering the woods, others firing from the other side of the river.

The emblem on Sitting Bull's shield, shown in this drawing by the great Sioux leader (upper), is based on images his father saw in a dream. This is the shield Sitting Bull gave to his nephew One Bull during the Reno attack. The bloodstained U.S. flag was found on the Custer battlefield on June 28, 1876. Each company had a flag like this to mark its position.

35

Major Reno gathered his men in an open parklike area surrounded by trees, with some men mounted and others standing beside their horses. Custer's favorite Arikara scout, Bloody Knife, stood about eight feet in front of Reno, and the white scout George Herendeen sat on his horse to Reno's right. "There was little firing for some minutes," Herendeen recalled, "and then we received a volley from the bushes. . . . The volley killed Bloody Knife and one soldier. I heard the soldier call out as he fell, 'Oh! My God, I have got it.'"

Bloody Knife's brains and blood splattered across Reno's face. He ordered his men to dismount so they could fight. Then, either out of panic or because he realized their best chance was to retreat, Reno quickly ordered them to remount. "The men scattered," said Herendeen, "getting out of the woods the best they could." This is when the serious killing began.

Wooden Leg—who had been asleep on the riverbank at the time of the attack—was late arriving at the battle and was near the river when the soldiers suddenly broke out of the woods. At first he thought the soldiers were attacking, and he and his companions quickly turned their horses and fled. But they soon realized that the bluecoats were running away, heading for a ford in the river.

"We whipped our ponies into swift pursuit. The soldier horses moved slowly, as if they were tired. Ours were lively. We gained rapidly on them. I fired four shots with my six shooter. . . . I saw a Sioux put an arrow into the back of a soldier's head. Another arrow went into his shoulder. He tumbled from his horse to the ground. Others fell dead either from arrows or from stabbings or jabbings or from blows by the stone war clubs of the Sioux. Horses limped or staggered or sprawled out dead or dying."

Wooden Leg captured a carbine from one soldier and headed for the river, where the fight turned into a wild, wet mass of Indians and whites thrashing in the cold water. Wielding his carbine like a war club, the young Cheyenne knocked two soldiers into the river. One Bull was there, too, killing two soldiers in the river and one on the other side.

While some Indians continued to pursue Reno's men up the steep hill on the eastern side of the river, others, including Black Elk, went among the dead

Bloody Knife

bodies of those left behind. "I was very small, and I had no chance to shoot anyone. . . . We stopped on a flat and everyone would get a soldier and strip him and put on his clothes for himself. We took everything they had—pistols, guns, ammunition, etc. . . . we saw a kicking soldier and a man came up and said, 'Boy, get off and scalp him.' So I got off and began to take my knife. Of course the soldier had short hair so I started to cut it off. Probably it hurt him because he began to grind his teeth. After I did this I took my pistol out and shot him in the forehead."

Wooden Leg found prizes among the dead as well: tobacco and cartridges for his new carbine. "Now I felt very brave. I jumped on my horse and went again to fight whatever soldiers I might find on the east side of the river." He rode up the hill toward Reno's men and fired a few shots but was soon distracted by a new threat to the village. "I had only been there a short time when somebody said to me, 'Look! Yonder are other soldiers!' I saw them on distant hills down the river and on our same side of it. The news of them spread quickly among us."

From the top of the hill, Reno's surviving men watched in amazement as the Indians began to ride off toward the south. "The fire and pursuit of the Indians seemed to cease as soon we reached the top of the bluffs," Private Taylor recalled. "This was much to be thankful for although we little dreamed of the cause."

Here, Wooden Leg steals a carbine (a shorter rifle used by the cavalry) from a soldier. "I whacked the white man fighter on his head with the heavy elk-horn handle of my pony whip," he recalled. "As I was getting possession of this weapon he fell to the ground. I did not harm him further." The weapons and ammunition captured from Reno's men made the Indians even stronger in the fight against Custer.

In one of the most accurate paintings of the final moments on Custer Hill,
artist Mort Künstler shows soldiers being overrun by Indian warriors. Custer
(top, near the American flag) appears as he looked on the day of the battle,
with short hair, buckskin pants, and a blue shirt.

the custer battle

After sending Reno to attack the village, Custer led his own men across a narrow fork of the creek and headed for higher ground, staying on the opposite side of the river from the Indian camp. One of his soldiers, Sergeant Daniel Kanipe, recalled: "[We] charged up the bluffs on the banks of the Little Big Horn. . . . When we reached the top . . . we were in plain view of the Indian camp. . . . Reno and his troops were seen to our left, charging at full speed down the valley. At sight of the camp, the boys began to cheer. Some horses became so excited that some riders were unable to hold them in ranks, and the last words I heard Custer say were, 'Hold your horses in, boys; there are plenty of them down there for all of us.'"

"Plenty" was an understatement. There were about three warriors for every man in Custer's regiment, and he had divided the regiment into four parts: his own battalion on the bluffs, Reno's in the valley, Benteen's somewhere back on the trail, and the slow-moving pack train under Captain McDougall, which carried extra ammunition that would be necessary for a major battle. Custer did not grasp the size of the village, because he could not see the whole village from this hill—the same hill where Reno would be driven in defeat less than an hour later. In fact, Custer never saw the whole village, and he would only recognize its true power as the Indians came out to fight.

At the moment, it looked like Reno was launching a successful attack, so Custer decided to continue riding north, looking for a place to cross the river and attack the village directly, to squeeze the Indians between his own force and Reno's. As they rode, Captain Tom Custer, the colonel's brother, sent Sergeant Kanipe back to find the pack train. He was to tell Captain McDougall to hurry and cut off any packs that came loose, unless they were ammunition packs. "And if you see Benteen," said Captain Custer, "tell him to come on quick—a big Indian camp."

Sergeant Daniel Kanipe

Examining cartridges found on the battlefield to determine if they were fired by Indians or soldiers helps experts reconstruct the action.

Captain George Yates

Captain Myles Keogh

Pretty White Buffalo

Some 20 minutes later, shortly after climbing another, higher hill that gave him a better view, Custer returned to his troops, who were gathered at the head of a dry gulch called Medicine Tail Coulee. From there he sent a trumpeter, John Martin, with a more urgent message for Captain Benteen. Martin, whose real name was Giovanni Martini, was from Italy, and his English was poor, so one of Custer's officers quickly scribbled out the message: "Benteen. Come on. Big Village. Be quick. Bring packs. P.[S.] bring pacs."

Custer now led his men down Medicine Tail Coulee toward the Little Bighorn River. About this time, his younger brother Boston, who was with the expedition as a civilian, arrived from the rear with news that he had passed Benteen a few miles back.

With Boston's arrival, Custer knew that Benteen was not far behind and naturally assumed that the captain would obey his order to hurry and bring the ammunition packs. So he stalled for time. Then his chief of scouts, Mitch Boyer, who had been watching the valley below, brought bad news: Reno's battalion had been defeated and was fleeing desperately across the river. Now there was no question of attacking the village—not until Benteen and the pack train arrived. So Custer decided to try a fake attack that would draw the Indians away from Reno.

He divided his command—now about 210 men—into two wings, one under Captain George Yates, the other under Captain Myles Keogh. While Keogh's troops stayed on a ridge above the coulee, Yates and his men thundered down toward the river. Many years later a Lakota woman named Pretty White Buffalo, cousin of Sitting Bull and wife of a Lakota warrior, described the attack and her belief that the village was protected by a higher power: "From across the river I could hear the music of the bugle and could see the column of soldiers turn to the left, to march down to the river to where the attack was to be made. All I could see was the warriors of my people. They rushed like the wind through the village, going down the ravine as the women went out to the grazing ground to round up the ponies. It was done very quickly. There had been no council the night before . . . and our camp was not pitched anticipating a

battle . . . what was done that day was done while the sun stood still and the white men were delivered into the hands of the Sioux."

Lakota and Cheyenne warriors chase Yates's men up Deep Coulee after their fake attack on the village, in this painting by Martin Pate.

Yates's attack did exactly what Custer intended, but it also brought a steady stream of warriors across the river to defend the village against this new threat. An Oglala leader named Low Dog, who was fighting Reno when he learned of the attack by Custer's men, recalled his surprise and strong commitment as he realized that there was another attack on his people. "They come on us like a thunderbolt. I never before nor since saw men so brave and fearless as those white warriors. We retreated until our men got all together, and then we charged upon them. I called to my men, 'This is a good day to die: follow me.' We massed our men, and that no man should fall back, every man whipped another man's horse and we rushed right upon them."

It took time for the warriors from the Reno battle to respond, so the first Indian resistance was light, and the Yates wing was able to fight their way back to join the other soldiers on the ridge with the loss of only one or two men. In the meantime, Keogh's men had been skirmishing with about 50 warriors who

Low Dog

41

had slipped out of the village the night before, eager for battle even before they knew the whites were coming.

Still strong, the combined forces moved to the next high point to the north, now called Calhoun Hill after Custer's brother-in-law Lieutenant James Calhoun, who commanded Company L in Keogh's wing. Even now, Custer was confident, for he took the Yates wing on a scouting mission farther north, while the Keogh wing was left to defend Calhoun Hill. Custer was probably looking for another place to cross the river and capture the women, children, and elders who were now fleeing in terror.

On Calhoun Hill, the men of Company L got off their horses and formed a skirmish line, while the other two companies, C and I, were held in reserve. Two Moons, who led a group of Cheyenne warriors while Gall and another chief named Crow King led the Hunkpapa, recalled that "a bugle sounded, and they all got off horses, and some soldiers led the horses over the hill. Then the Sioux rode up the ridge on all sides, riding very fast. The Cheyenne went up the left way."

At first the Indians fought cautiously, shooting from a distance. Although some had rifles or carbines—including those captured in the Reno battle— many used traditional bows and arrows, which they loosed in long, high arcs so that they could stay hidden in the gullies. The cavalrymen shot back carefully, following orders and keeping the Indians away. Antelope Woman was somewhere below Calhoun Hill, looking for her nephew Noisy Walking, who had taken the suicide vow the night before. She had not yet found her nephew, but she clearly described a turning point in the battle, when Company C tried a disastrous charge:

By hiding in gullies, Indians could shoot their arrows without being seen by the soldiers.

"A band of the soldiers on the ridge mounted their horses and came riding in a gallop down the broad coulee toward the river. . . . Lame White Man, the bravest Cheyenne warrior chief, stayed in hiding close where the small band of soldiers got off their horses. From there he called to the young men, and they began creeping and dodging back to him. The Ogallala Sioux chiefs also called to their young men. . . . Within a few minutes there were many hundreds of warriors wriggling along the gullies all around those soldiers. . . . After a little while I heard Lame White Man call out: 'Young men, come now with me and show yourselves to be brave!'"

Lame White Man led the young warriors in a charge that wiped out much of Company C and chased the survivors back to Calhoun Hill. The chief himself was killed in the fighting that followed, but his charge marked the beginning of the end for Custer's troops. Keogh's wing began to fall apart and scatter desperately into a lower "saddle" in the land to the north. Here another charge broke their resistance further.

Lame White Man

One Bull, who led the battle against Reno, had been ordered by his uncle to stay out of the fighting with Custer, because Sitting Bull saw the blood of Good Bear Boy, who had been rescued by One Bull in the Reno battle. His older brother White Bull, however, was in the middle of the action, side by side with the great Lakota war chief Crazy Horse. White Bull later claimed that he challenged Crazy Horse to charge through the soldiers, but Crazy Horse "backed out." According to White Bull, he then "went on the run [and] rode thru . . . leaning on top of

This 1873 Winchester repeating rifle was used by an Indian warrior at the Battle of Little Bighorn.

the horse, leaning down." Most Indians, however, remembered that it was Crazy Horse who led the charge that divided the rest of Keogh's soldiers.

There were probably several brave charges at this point in the battle, by White Bull, Crazy Horse, and others. These charges were not only a display of courage, but also a sound military tactic, for the soldiers shot at the charger with their single-shot rifles, and before they could reload, the Indians would rush in for hand-to-hand combat. Crazy Horse's brother-in-law Red Feather, who was with him that day, later said:

"The Indians hid behind little rolls. The soldiers were on one side of the hill and the Indians on the other, a slight rise between them. While they were lying there shooting at one another, Crazy Horse came up on horseback—with an eagle horn—and rode between the two parties. The soldiers all fired at once, but didn't hit him. The Indians got the idea the soldiers' guns were empty and charged immediately on the soldiers."

Wielding war clubs, hatchets, and sharp knives, swinging their rifles and bows, the warriors wiped out most of Keogh's wing, including Captain Keogh himself. The survivors made their way to the far end of the ridge, now called Custer Hill or Last Stand Hill, where the large white monument stands in mute testimony to those who died there.

Around the same time that the Indians were destroying Keogh's wing, the Yates wing—which had returned from its scout with Custer—was fighting hard in a bowl-like area below Last Stand Hill. One of the two companies in the wing, Company E, had all gray horses and was remembered by many Indians, who spoke of their bravery and toughness under fire. "I could not break the line at the bunch of gray horses," said Two Moons.

According to Cheyenne historian John Stands in Timber—who heard the story from his grandfather, a Cheyenne leader named Wolf Tooth—it was the suicide boys who broke the stiff resistance of the gray-horse troop, galloping up

Privates Timothy Donnelly (left) and George Walker (right) pose not long before the battle. Both were killed with Custer.

from the river, stampeding the soldiers' horses and throwing themselves into battle: "The suicide boys started the hand-to-hand fighting, and all of them were killed or mortally wounded. When the soldiers started shooting at them, the Indians above with Wolf Tooth came in from the other side. Then there was no time for them to take aim or anything. The Indians were right behind and among them. . . . At the end it was quite a mess. They could not tell which was this man or that man, it was so mixed up."

It may have been in the middle of this "mixed up" fighting that White Bull

This popular 1896 lithograph contributed to misinformation about the battle. Custer is inaccurately shown with long hair and a saber (the Seventh Cavalry left their sabers behind), and Indians look more like African warriors than Plains Indians.

jumped off his horse and charged toward a tall, well-built soldier. "He threw his rifle at me without shooting," White Bull recalled. "I dodged it. We grabbed each other and wrestled there in the dust and smoke. . . . He hit me with his fists on the jaw and shoulders, then grabbed my long braids with both hands, pulled my face close and tried to bite my nose off. . . . Finally, I broke free. He drew his pistol. I wrenched it out of his hand and struck him with it three or four times on the head, knocked him over, shot him in the head and fired at his heart."

The survivors, perhaps a hundred men in all, some of them badly wounded, gathered together on Last Stand Hill. More than a thousand Indian warriors surrounded them, some still shooting from the gullies, others riding around the doomed men in ever-tightening circles. Two Moons vividly described the scene:

"Then the shooting was quick, quick. Pop—pop—pop very fast. Some of the soldiers were down on their knees, some standing. Officers all in front. The smoke was like a great cloud, and everywhere the Sioux went the dust rose like

James Calhoun Tom Custer George Custer Autey Reed Boston Custer

smoke. We circled all around them—swirling like water round a stone. We shoot, we ride fast, we shoot again. Soldiers drop, and horses fall on them."

The soldiers on the hill died quickly, no more than a half hour from the attack of the suicide boys until it was over. Toward the end, a group of desperate men made a mad dash for the river, running down the long slope and into a deep ravine, where the last of them were killed. This may have been the end of the battle, but Indian accounts suggest that a few men were still alive on the hill—or at least one man. Wooden Leg, who had spent much of the battle firing from a distance, recalled the final moments as he and others charged the hill:

"It appeared that all of the white men were dead. But there was one of them who raised himself to a support on his left elbow. He turned and looked over his left shoulder, and then I got a good view of him. His expression was wild, as if his mind was all tangled up and he was wondering what was going on here. In his right hand he held his six-shooter. Many of the Indians near him were scared by what seemed to have been a return from death to life. But a Sioux warrior jumped forward, grabbing the six-shooter and wrenched it from the soldier's grasp. The gun was turned upon the white man, and he was shot in the head. Other Indians struck him or stabbed him. I think he must have been the last man killed in this great battle where not one of the enemy got away."

Five members of the Custer family died at Little Bighorn: Tom, George, and Boston were brothers; James Calhoun was their brother-in-law; and Autey Reed was their nephew. While the three older men were professional soldiers, Boston and Autey, both just 17 years old, joined the Little Bighorn campaign as civilians, thinking it would be a summer of fun and adventure.

As he chases a trooper up Reno Hill, an Indian warrior shows his skill at being able to ride and use both hands to shoot his rifle. Soldiers tended to keep one hand on the reins, which made them slower and less accurate when firing.

Major Marcus Reno's dazed and exhausted men reached the top of the bluffs, called Reno Hill today, just as the Custer battle was beginning downstream. "Major Reno was walking around in an excited manner," wrote Private William Taylor. "He had lost his hat . . . and had bound a red handkerchief about his head, which gave him a rather peculiar and unmilitary appearance. Most of the men had thrown themselves on the ground to rest for they were well nigh exhausted."

Reno himself rode southward a short distance to meet Captain Benteen, who showed him the note from Custer: "Benteen. Come on. Big Village. Be quick. Bring packs. P.[S.] bring pacs." There have been many questions as to why Reno and Benteen did not make more of an effort to "be quick" and bring the ammunition. Benteen's slowness is difficult to explain, but Reno's men had used up much of their ammunition in the valley fight, and he sent an officer back to hurry the pack train. In the meantime, he was concerned with protecting his own men, caring for the wounded, and burying the dead.

Reno had lost 3 officers and 29 enlisted men in the brutal valley fight, with 7 wounded and many others missing. One of these, the Arikara scout Young Hawk, was trapped with 5 other Arikaras and 1 Crow scout in a grove of trees on the eastern bank of the Little Bighorn.

Two scouts were badly wounded, and Young Hawk recalled his feelings of desperation: "The sight of the wounded men gave me queer feelings, I did not want to see them mutilated, so I decided to get killed myself at the edge of the timber. Before going out I put my arms about my horse's neck, saying, 'I love you.' I then crawled out and stood up and saw all in front of me Sioux warriors kneeling ready to shoot. I fired at them and received a volley but was not hit."

Young Hawk killed two Lakota warriors and a handsome gray horse that one of the warriors rode. Shortly after this, he saw that the Sioux and Cheyenne were leaving—to fight Custer, as he later learned. "After the

Captain Frederick Benteen

Young Hawk

Captain Thomas Weir

*Lieutenant
Winfield Edgerly*

shooting had slackened, I stood up and looked around. On the ridge above me on the highest point I saw a United States flag." Young Hawk cut a stick and tied a white handkerchief to it. He and the others got the two wounded scouts on their horses, and they all rode up the hill to join the soldiers.

By the time Young Hawk and his group reached the hilltop, the soldiers had been hearing firing in the distance. One of Benteen's company commanders, Captain Thomas Weir, decided to lead his men northward to see what was happening with Custer. Weir did not receive permission, but over the next 45 minutes, all of the other companies would follow his lead. During this time the pack train finally arrived, allowing Reno's men to replenish their ammunition.

Captain Weir reached the crest of a higher hill, called Weir Point today, about a mile and a quarter north, where he could see the Custer battlefield in the distance. His second-in-command, Lieutenant Winfield Edgerly, later testified: "When we got on the ridge, we saw a good many Indians riding up and down firing at objects on the ground. They saw us about the same time we saw them."

Most historians have assumed that what Weir and Edgerly saw was the end of the Custer battle on Last Stand Hill. But it is possible that they were actually watching the end of the first phase of the battle, when Lame White Man's charge led to the destruction of Company C on Calhoun Hill. Either way, the soldiers were forced to turn back just as men under Captain Benteen arrived. "We had not been more than 2 or 3 minutes at that high point," Benteen recalled, "before the gorge was filled with Indians rushing towards us."

Upon receiving word of the new threat, Major Reno ordered the entire command to fall back to their original position on Reno Hill. Company K, under Lieutenant Edward Godfrey, bravely dismounted and formed a skirmish line to hold off the attackers while the other companies established positions in a rough horseshoe shape along two parallel ridges, with the wounded men and pack animals in a lower area in the center.

Private Charles Windolph, under Benteen's command in Company H, recalled the first furious moments under fire: "We hurriedly piled up such inadequate barricades as we could find. We used pack saddles, boxes of hard tack, and bacon, anything we could lay our hands on. . . . We'd hardly got settled down on our skirmish line, with "H" men posted at twenty-feet intervals, when the Indians had us all but completely surrounded, and the fighting began in earnest. There was no full-fledged charge, but little groups of Indians would creep up as close as they could get, and from behind bushes or little knolls open fire. They'd practice all kinds of cute tricks to draw our fire."

The "cute tricks" and steady pounding from Indian sharpshooters took a toll, killing 18 enlisted men and wounding 46 by the time the firing died down with the coming of darkness. The soldiers labored through the night, digging rifle pits and strengthening their fortifications with dead horses and mules. The dead were buried in shallow graves near the living.

Private Windolph eloquently described the strange uncertainty of the dark Montana night: "The sun went down that night like a ball of fire. Pretty soon the quick Montana twilight settled down on us, and then came the chill of the

Private
Charles Windolph

Captain Thomas Weir and his men gaze across the rolling landscape to see Indians "firing at objects on the ground" in this Martin Pate painting. Those "objects" were Custer's men, but Weir and his company had little time to analyze the situation before Indians drove them back toward Reno Hill.

high plains. There was no moon, and no one ever welcomed darkness more than we did.

"The firing had gradually died out. Now and again you'd hear the ping of a rifle bullet, but by 10 o'clock even that had stopped. But welcome as the darkness was, it brought a penetrating feeling of fear and uncertainty of what tomorrow might bring. We felt terribly alone on that dangerous hilltop. We were a million miles from nowhere. And death was all around us."

While the soldiers waited uneasily on the lonely hilltop, three Crow scouts slipped past the Sioux and Cheyenne and rode through the darkness northward along the Little Bighorn. These three—Goes Ahead, Hairy Moccasin, and White Man Runs Him—had been with Custer as far as Medicine Tail Coulee, where they were sent back by Custer's chief of scouts, Mitch Boyer, who told them they had done their job by finding the village, and they should leave the fighting to the soldiers. Although the Crow did not yet know for sure what had

White Man Runs Him

happened to Custer, they had seen enough to believe that he and his soldiers had all been killed. They were the first to bring word of the battle to Custer's commanding officer, General Alfred Terry, whom the Indians called "No-Hip-Bone" because he walked with a limp.

Years later, White Man Runs Him, spoke of why he helped the soldiers and how he felt that night as he carried word of the horrible battle: "I endured all the hardships the soldiers endured in order to hold my land. . . . They did not know the country. I did. They wanted me for their eye, they could not see. . . . Had Custer not ordered me to go, the people who visit the Custer Field to-day would see my name on the monument. . . . Custer and the soldiers were my friends and companions, and I cried all night long as I rode through the rain to tell No-Hip-Bone the news."

General Terry was camped a full day's march north of the battlefield, so there would be no immediate relief for the men on Reno Hill. The fighting started again at dawn. "The first thing I heard was two rifle shots," said Major Reno, "and as everything was quiet, at that time, it was something that attracted attention. It was immediately succeeded by firing from all round the position." Reno was a battle-hardened officer who had served in the Civil War, but he called the firing that morning "as severe as I ever experienced."

As the day grew warmer, the wounded men cried out desperately for water. The Little Bighorn was just below them, but the Indians guarded it, knowing the soldiers would be forced to surrender without water. Captain Benteen called for volunteers to go for water, and several were wounded as they scrambled down to the river and back. Then Benteen posted four expert marksman, including Private Windolph, to cover the water carriers. "We were to stand up and not only draw the fire from the Indians below," Windolph remembered, "but we were to pump as much lead as we could into the bushes where the Indians were hiding, while the water party hurried down to the draw, got their buckets and pots and canteens filled, and then made their way back." Twenty-four men, including Windolph, received the Medal of Honor for their bravery on Reno Hill.

General Alfred Terry

Private Windolph's Medal of Honor

The heavy firing began to die down in the late morning, but Indian sharpshooters kept the men pinned to their positions all afternoon. Finally, late in the afternoon, the firing stopped completely, and the Little Bighorn valley below filled with smoke as the Indians set fire to the grass to cover their movements. Down in the timber where Reno's men had first retreated, a civilian interpreter named Fred Girard—who had been caught in the timber now for more than 24 hours—had a close-up view of the Indian village moving south toward the Bighorn Mountains. "The great horde of warriors and ponies and squaws and children passed so near to us that we could plainly see wounded warriors on travois and dead warriors thrown across and tied to the backs of horses. Above all the noise and rattle and the hum of voices and cries of children we could hear the death chanting of the squaws."

General Terry arrived on the hilltop early the next morning, June 27. It was the approach of Terry's soldiers that convinced the Indians to move their village. They had lost too many warriors and used too much ammunition to fight another large battle. Terry had passed the Custer battlefield on the way to Reno Hill, and he informed the men that Custer's entire command had been killed. Captain Benteen rode off that afternoon to look at the battlefield, while Reno supervised the movement of his 59 wounded men down from the hill to Terry's camp in the valley. A total of 53 men had been killed in the valley and hilltop fights; most of them were buried in rifle pits on the hill.

Burials on the Custer field did not begin until the following day, Wednesday, June 28, three days after the battle, when Reno led the surviving men of the Seventh Cavalry to the battlefield. "I thought that was a proper duty for the 7th," he later said, that we should take care of the wounded and bury our comrades because we would be best able to recognize them."

Private William Taylor, who was with the burial detail, described his first view of the horrible scene. "The actual field of battle was less than one mile in length and perhaps one half mile in width, the main part being on a ridge that ran nearly parallel with the river and about a mile from it. Most of the bodies were on the slope of the ridge but there were quite a number scattered

A pile of bleached horse bones on Custer Hill in 1877 attests to the many animals that were killed in the general fighting. Some desperate troopers killed their own horses in order to form a protective "breastworks" against the Indians.

between the river and the ridge, and how white they looked at a distance, like little mounds of snow."

Many men commented on the whiteness of the bodies, for they had been stripped naked by the Indians, who took clothing and other possessions as the spoils of battle. Custer's body was found on Last Stand Hill, close to his brother Tom, with bullet wounds in his left temple and near his heart. He was not scalped—perhaps because of his short hair—but there was blood coming from his ears. Those who found him believed this was caused by the head wound.

Years later, Antelope Woman offered a different explanation that she heard from two Cheyenne women who knew Custer from an earlier time when he promised their chiefs he would never attack the Cheyenne again: "The women . . . pushed the point of a sewing awl into each of his ears, into his head. This was done to improve his hearing, as it seemed he had not heard what our chiefs in the South said when he smoked the pipe with them. They told him then that if ever afterward he should break that peace promise and should fight the Cheyennes the Everywhere Spirit surely would cause him to be killed."

Sitting Bull, a prisoner-of-war at Fort Randall in 1882, sits with Four Robes, the younger of his two wives, and three of their children. The white woman and child are unidentified, as is the soldier.

News of the Battle of Little Bighorn first reached the outside world on July 5, 1876, the day after the nation's joyous celebration of the 100th anniversary of American independence. The embarrassing defeat of Custer, one of America's most famous and popular soldiers, drove the government to quick and ruthless action. By the end of July, Congress had approved funds to build two new forts on the Yellowstone River and add 2,500 cavalry troopers. Control of the Sioux agencies was given to the army. On August 15, all food and rations for the Sioux at the agencies was cut off. It was "sign or starve," and the agency Indians had no choice but to sign away their rights to the Black Hills.

Now the army went after the hunting bands. By this time, the great village of Sitting Bull had broken up into smaller groups, because they could not find enough grass, food, and firewood to keep so many people together. From the summer of 1876 through the winter and spring of 1877, army forces relentlessly pursued the Lakota and Cheyenne, destroying their villages and their food supplies. They were faced with an even more painful choice than the agency Indians: "surrender or starve."

In early May 1877, Crazy Horse led 889 Lakota and Cheyenne to surrender at Fort Robinson in Nebraska, while Sitting Bull led about a thousand followers across the border into Canada. Crazy Horse struggled with reservation life, and other leaders were jealous of his power. That September, he pulled out a knife as he was being taken to the guardhouse at Fort Robinson. In the struggle, he was killed by a soldier's bayonet.

Many of Crazy Horse's followers joined Sitting Bull in Canada for a time, but as the buffalo herds grew smaller, the Indians gradually returned to the American agencies for food. Finally, in 1881, Sitting Bull and 187 followers surrendered at Fort Buford in what is now North Dakota. After two years as a military prisoner, he settled near the Standing Rock Agency, where the Indian agent considered him an obstacle to "progress."

In 1890, a new spiritual movement called the Ghost Dance caught fire among the Lakota, and the agent used it as an excuse to arrest Sitting Bull. On December 15, 1890, Sitting Bull and seven followers were killed by Indian policemen sent to arrest him. Two weeks later, the Seventh Cavalry killed 146 Lakota, including 44 women and children, at a creek called Wounded Knee. It was the last, sad episode of the Indian wars.

TIME LINE OF BATTLES FOR INDIAN LAND

The Battle of Little Bighorn was one of many battles between whites and Indians in what is now the United States. Although whites often described the reasons for these conflicts in terms of culture, or religion, or "civilization," the real issue was land. These time lines and maps illustrate some key battles, treaties, and other events that took place as the demands of an ever-growing white population for more land clashed with the desire of Native Americans to hold onto their homelands and traditional lifestyle.

The focus here is on settlers moving west from the 13 British colonies, which became the United States. However, there were also many conflicts between the Spanish and Indians in Mexico and what is now the American Southwest, as well as

between the British and Indians in Canada. The French played an important role until 1763, but because they were more interested in trade, they generally fought with Indian allies against the British rather than fighting directly against the Indians for land.

Here is an interesting fact to consider: In 1500, around the time the first Europeans arrived, there were between one million and seven million Indian people living in what is now the United States and Canada. Today, there are almost 300 million people in the continental United States, and we're all living on land that used to belong to the Indians. The map of present-day reservations below shows the small areas of land that the U.S. government recognizes today as belonging to American Indians.

1607 First permanent English settlement in present-day United States is established at Jamestown, Virginia.

1622 The Powhatan Confederacy attacks Jamestown, killing 347 men, women, and children. Three years later, colonists kill a thousand Indians in the village of Pamunkey. Hostilities continue off and on until 1646.

1626 Dutch purchase Manhattan Island (site of New York City) from local Indians for 60 guilders worth of trade goods.

1636–37 Pequot Indians and New England settlers fight a series of battles. On May 27, 1637, white settlers attack a Pequot village, killing more than 600 men, women, and children.

1675–76 King Philip's War ends with the death of the Wampanoag sachem (chief), Metacom, called King Philip by the colonists. His death ends Indian conflicts in New England.

1689–1763 Series of wars between the British and their Iroquois allies and the French and their Algonquian allies for control of North America: King William's War (1689–97), Queen Anne's War (1702–13), King George's War (1744–48); French and Indian War (1754–63).

1711–13 Tuscarora Indians are defeated by British settlers in North Carolina.

1715 British colonists drive the Yamassee out of South Carolina, opening land to white settlement.

1760–61 Battles between the Cherokee and British soldiers ca the Cherokee to give up much of eastern lands in Virginia, the Carolinas, and Georgia.

1763–64 Ottawa chief Pontiac l a confederacy that destroys eig British forts and kills hundreds o settlers and soldiers before colla in the fall of 1764.

October 7, 1763 After Britain's v in the French and Indian War, K George III establishes the Proclamation Line, which prohib white settlers from moving acro Appalachians onto Indian land.

1774 Virginia's governor (Lord Dunsmore) violates the Proclam of 1763 by granting land west of Appalachians to soldiers who s in the French and Indian War. B fighting forces the Shawnee ou Kentucky.

1778–79 The power of the Iroqu Confederacy ends when Americ destroy Indian villages in weste New York and Pennsylvania.

1787 Northwest Ordinance establishes government for terr northwest of the Ohio River; pro protection of tribal lands but als paves the way for white settlem

1789 U.S. Constitution gives the federal government, rather than states, the power to make treati with Indian tribes.

Present-Day Reservations

1607-1789

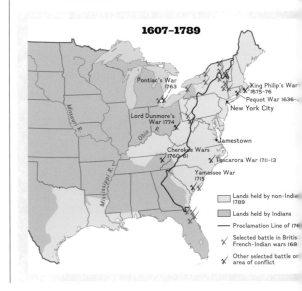

Miami chief Little Turtle and his ...ederacy defeat General Arthur ...air, winning the largest single ...ry in the Indian Wars on ...mber 2.

... Power of the Miami ...ederacy is broken on August 20 ...merican forces led by General ...d Anthony" Wayne at the Battle ...len Timbers in present-day Ohio.

...st 3, 1795 Warriors and chiefs ...ding Little Turtle) representing ...bes sign the Treaty of Greenville, ...ing to give up most of present-...Ohio as well as part of Indiana.

... Louisiana Purchase brings ... legislation allowing eastern ... to trade their land for land west ... Mississippi. During the next 25 ..., some Indian groups voluntarily ... to the new territory.

... At Fort Wayne, Indiana, ...nor William Henry Harrison ... drunken Indians into signing ... almost three million acres in ...nt-day Indiana and Illinois.

...-1811 Shawnee chief Tecumseh ... Indian resistance to settlement ... area defined by Treaty of Fort ...e. The rebellion ends at ...canoe when William Henry ...son's troops defeat warriors led ...cumseh's brother.

...18 Andrew Jackson invades ...sh Florida to fight Seminoles in ...rst Seminole War.

...1824 Most Kickapoo bands are ...ved from Illinois and Indiana;

Kenekuk, the "Kickapoo Prophet," uses nonviolent resistance to keep his people on their traditional land until 1832.

1825 Region west of Arkansas and Missouri and east of Mexican Territory is officially defined by the U.S. government as "Indian Country."

May 26, 1830 Indian Removal Act, which will lead to the forced removal of eastern tribes to lands west of the Mississippi, is passed.

1831-39 The removal of the Five Civilized Tribes—Cherokee, Choctaw, Chickasaw, Creek, and Seminole—to territory in present-day Oklahoma culminates in the Trail of Tears 1838–1839.

1832 Sauk and Fox tribes under Black Hawk are defeated at Bad Axe River on August 2 and forced to give up land in Illinois, Wisconsin, and Iowa.

1835-42 The Second Seminole War is fought as Seminoles continue to resist removal to the west.

1846-48 Increased migration on the Oregon Trail leads to clashes with the Indians; the Cayuse kill 14 whites, including Dr. Marcus Whitman and his wife, Narcissa, at the Whitman Mission on November 29, 1847.

1848-49 Gold discovery brings more than 100,000 whites to California during the first year, overrunning Indian lands in California and increasing friction on overland trails.

Selected Battles, Treaties, and Other Key Events 1850-1890

1851 Treaty of Fort Laramie defines territory for Northern Plains tribes and promises annual payments of goods and supplies in return for Indians' promise to allow the government "to establish roads, military and other posts" in their territory.

August 1854 Warfare between the Lakota and U.S. government begins when a cow is killed on the Oregon Trail near Fort Laramie.

1861-1886 Apache bands in Arizona and New Mexico under leaders such as Mangas Coloradas, Cochise, Victorio, and Geronimo resist white intrusion and forced removal to reservations. Geronimo surrenders to General George Crook in 1886.

1862 Starving Santee Sioux led by Little Crow kill 400–800 whites in Minnesota before being defeated at Wood Lake. Little Crow escapes, but 38 warriors are executed in the largest mass hanging in U.S. history.

1863-68 Troops under Kit Carson force more than 8,000 Navajo to make the "Long Walk" from their homeland in northern Arizona to the Bosque Redondo Reservation in eastern New Mexico. They are allowed to return to Arizona in 1868.

November 29, 1864 Colorado militia attacks a peaceful Cheyenne and Arapaho village at Sand Creek, killing about 150 Indians, mostly women, children, and old men.

1866-68 Attacks by Red Cloud and his Lakota and Cheyenne warriors on forts protecting the Bozeman Trail to

Montana's goldfields include the massacre of 80 soldiers near Ft. Phil Kearny by warriors under Crazy Horse.

1867-69 Custer's attack on Cheyenne village on the Washita River is one of several campaigns that put an end to Southern Cheyenne resistance.

1868 In new treaties signed at Fort Laramie with the Sioux, Cheyenne, and Arapaho, the U.S. agrees to close forts on the Bozeman Trail, establish the Great Sioux Reservation *(see map p. 14)*, and preserve the tribes' right to hunt in the Powder River country.

1874-76 Gold discovery in the Black Hills brings thousands of miners illegally onto the Great Sioux Reservation.

1876-1877 Lakota and Northern Cheyenne resist U.S. demands to report to reservations, igniting the Great Sioux War. They win at Little Bighorn but are defeated in other battles. They are forced to give up their rights to the Black Hills.

1881 Sitting Bull and 187 followers surrender at Fort Buford.

1889 A large part of Indian Territory (present-day Oklahoma) is opened to white settlers.

1890 The Ghost Dance, an Indian religious movement, causes fear among whites. On December 29, 146 Lakota, including 44 women and 18 children, are killed by U.S. soldiers at Wounded Knee on the Pine Ridge Reservation, in South Dakota.

Battle of Little Bighorn

SUNDAY, JUNE 25, 1876
The times in bold are estimated sun time at the battlefield. The Seventh Cavalry used Chicago time (in parentheses), which was 80 minutes later than sun time at the battlefield.

Dawn
Village first seen by Crow scouts.

7:40 AM (9:00 AM)
Custer sees "cloud-like" objects that scouts tell him are pony herds.

9:30 AM (10:50 AM)
Custer tells officers he plans to attack.

10:40 AM (Noon)
Custer divides regiment into three battalions under himself, Reno, and Benteen, with McDougall assigned to guard the pack train.

1:25 PM (2:45 PM)
Custer tells Reno to charge the village.

1:45 PM (3:05 PM)
Reno's men charge the village.

1:55 PM (3:15 PM)
Custer sends message to Benteen and McDougall.

2:15 PM (3:35 PM)
Custer sends note to Benteen.

2:35 PM (3:55 PM)
Reno begins to retreat.

2:40 PM (4:00 PM)
Custer descends Medicine Tail Coulee; divides his command into two battalions under Keogh and Yates.

2:50 PM (4:10 PM)
Reno's men arrive on Reno Hill; Custer sends Yates to attack village; he and Keogh's battalion find higher ground.

3:00 PM (4:20 PM)
Yates's battalion attacks village; Benteen's battalion arrives at Reno Hill.

3:25 PM (4:45 PM)
Yates reunites with Keogh and Custer, and they move to Calhoun Hill; Keogh's battalion stays to defend the position; Custer and Yates scout farther north.

3:45 PM (5:05 PM)
Weir's company looks for Custer.

4:05 PM (5:25 PM)
Weir's group sees Indians firing at Custer's men.

4:15-4:50 PM (5:35–6:10 PM)
Indians advance on Weir Point; soldiers retreat to Reno Hill.

Dusk
Indian attack on Reno Hill ends with darkness.

1790-1849

Whitman Mission
Bad Axe
Ft. Wayne
Tippecanoe — Fallen Timbers
St. Clair's Defeat
Missouri R.
Ohio R.
Mississippi R.
First Seminole War
Second Seminole War

Lands held by non-Indians 1849
Lands held by Indians
✗ Selected battle or area of conflict
■ Fort

1850-1890

Little Bighorn 1876
Ft. Buford
Ft. Phil Kearny
Wood Lake 1862
Ft. Laramie
Wounded Knee 1890
Missouri R.
Sand Creek 1864
Washita River 1868
Apache Wars 1861-1886
Ft. Sumner (Bosque Redondo)
Ohio R.
Mississippi R.

Lands held by non-Indians 1890
Lands held by Indians
✗ Selected battle or area of conflict
■ Fort

selected sources

DeMallie, Raymond J., ed. *The Sixth Grandfather: Black Elk's Teachings Given to John G. Neihardt.* Lincoln: University of Nebraska Press, 1984.

Dixon, Joseph K. *The Vanishing Race.* NY: Bonanza Books, 1975, c.1913.

Fox, Richard Allan. *Archaeology, History, and Custer's Last Battle.* Norman: University of Oklahoma Press, 1993.

Graham, W.A. *The Custer Myth.* Mechanicsburg, PA: Stackpole Books, 1953. Revised edition, 1995.

Gray, John S. *Centennial Campaign.* Norman: University of Oklahoma Press, 1988.

_____. *Custer's Last Campaign.* Lincoln: University of Nebraska Press, 1991.

Greene, Jerome A., ed. *Lakota and Cheyenne.* Norman: University of Oklahoma Press, 1994.

Hammer, Kenneth. *Custer in '76.* Norman: University of Oklahoma Press, 1990.

Hardorff, Richard G., comp. and ed. *Indian Views of the Custer Fight.* Norman: University of Oklahoma Press, 2005.

_____. *Lakota Recollections of the Custer Fight.* Lincoln: University of Nebraska Press, 1997.

Libby, O.G., ed. *The Arikara Narrative of Custer's Campaign and the Little Bighorn.* Norman: University of Oklahoma Press, 1998. Originally published Bismarck: North Dakota Historical Society, 1920.

Marquis, Thomas B. "She Watched Custer's Last Battle, Her Story, Interpreted in 1927." Hardin, MT: Custer Battle Museum, 1935, in *Custer on the Little Bighorn.* Heil, Anna Rose Octavia, comp. and ed. Lodi, CA: End-Kian Publishing Co., 1967.

_____. *A Warrior Who Fought Custer.* Minneapolis: Midwest Company, 1931. Reprint. *Wooden Leg.* Lincoln: University of Nebraska Press, 1962.

Michno, Gregory F. *Lakota Noon.* Missoula, MT: Mountain Press Publishing Company, 1997.

Miller, David Humphreys. *Custer's Fall.* New York: Duell, Sloan and Pearce, 1957.

Nichols, Ronald H., comp. and ed. *Reno Court of Inquiry.* Hardin, MT: Custer Battlefield Historical & Museum Association, 1996.

Overfield, Lloyd J, II. *The Little Bighorn 1876.* Glendale, CA: The Arthur H. Clark Company, 1971.

Stands in Timber, John and Margot Liberty. *Cheyenne Memories.* New Haven: Yale University Press, 1967.

Taylor, William O. *With Custer on the Little Bighorn.* NY: Viking Penguin, 1996.

Utley, Robert M. *The Lance and the Shield.* NY: Henry Holt and Company, 1993.

Windolph, Charles. *I Fought with Custer.* As told to Frazier and Robert Hunt. NY: Scribner, 1950, c. 1947. Reprint. Lincoln: University of Nebraska Press, 1987.

quote sources

All quotes, with a few minor exceptions, are from primary sources, either as originally published or as published in a source anthology or other scholarly work.

For sources listed in Selected Sources, only author's last name and publication date where necessary are given.

All quotes from the following are from single sources listed in Selected Sources (above):

Wooden Leg: Marquis, 1931; Antelope Woman: Marquis, 1935; Black Elk: DeMallie; William Taylor: Taylor; Charles Windolph: Windolph; Young Hawk: Libby; John Stands in Timber: Stands in Timber; George Herendeen: Graham.

Other sources as follows, identified by text page number in bold and speaker.

11. Custer: Krause, Herbert and Gary D. Olson. *Prelude to Glory.* Sioux Falls: Brevet Press, 1976. **13.** Little Big Man: Lazarus, Edward. *Black Hills / White Justice.* NY: HarperCollins, 1991. **14.** Secretary of Interior (Zachariah Chandler): Gray, 1988. **17.** voice: Utley. **18.** Two Moons: Graham. **19.** soldier: Mears, David. "Campaigning Against Crazy Horse." Nebraska State Historical Society Publications XV (1907). **22–23.** Sitting Bull: Vestal, Stanley. *Sitting Bull.* Norman: University of Oklahoma Press, 1957. **24–25.** Varnum, Custer, and Boyer (from Varnum): Hammer. **26.** Custer (from Godfrey): Graham.

29. Custer's order (from Reno): Nichols. **30–31.** Petring: Hammer. **31.** Reno: Overfield; Gall: Graham. **32–34.** One Bull: (1st) Greene; (2nd & 3rd) Miller. **33.** White Bull and Sitting Bull: Hardorff, 2005. **39.** Kanipe: Gray, 1991; Tom Custer (from Kanipe): Hammer. **40.** note to Benteen: Graham (photo of note); Pretty White Buffalo (Mrs. Spotted Horn Bull): McLaughlin, James. *My Friend the Indian.* NY: Houghton Mifflin, 1910. Revised edition. Seattle: Superior Publishing, 1970.

41. Low Dog: Hardorff, 2005. **42.** Two Moons: Graham. **43–44.** White Bull: Hardorff, 1997. **44.** Red Feather: Hardorff, 1997; Two Moons: Dixon. **46.** White Bull: Vestal (for full reference see pp. 22–23). **46–47.** Two Moons: Graham. **50.** Edgerly & Benteen: Nichols. **53.** White Man Runs Him: Dixon. **53–54.** Reno: Nichols. **54.** Girard: Hammer. **Back Cover.** Custer: *My Life on the Plains.* New York: Sheldon and Company, 1874. (others on back cover as listed in main text).

selected postscripts

Antelope Woman, who became known as Kate Bighead, settled on the Northern Cheyenne Reservation in Montana and told her story to Dr. Thomas Marquis in 1927 *(see Selected Sources).*

Frederick Benteen, who was treated as a hero for his leadership on Reno Hill, remained critical of Custer until his death in 1898 at the age of 63.

Black Elk joined Buffalo Bill's Wild West show in 1886 and later became involved in the Ghost Dance on the Pine Ridge Reservation in South Dakota. He told his story to John Neihardt *(see Selected Sources).* Black Elk died at age 86 in 1950.

Fred Girard and **George Herendeen** continued to work as civilians for the army and were both critical of Reno at the official inquiry in 1879. Girard died in 1913 at age 83; Herendeen died in 1918 at age 75.

Little Big Man was involved in the struggle that resulted in Crazy Horse's death. It is unclear whether he was trying to stop his old friend from getting into trouble or whether he was part of a conspiracy to kill him.

One Bull and White Bull both served as Indian policemen and other official positions on reservations in South Dakota. Walter Stanley Campbell (Stanley Vestal) used their stories to create the first full biography of Sitting Bull *(see Quote Sources).* The brothers died within a month of each other in 1947.

Marcus Reno, accused by a Custer biographer of cowardice at Little Bighorn, requested a military inquiry, which cleared his name in 1879. A year later, he was dismissed from the army because of a different issue. Reno died in 1889 at the age of 54.

Thomas Weir was very critical of both Reno and Benteen for not doing more to aid Custer. He died in New York in 1876 (age 38) and was not available to testify at the Reno inquiry.

White Man Runs Him settled on the Crow Reservation in Montana, often attending events at the Little Bighorn Battlefield. He died in 1929 at the age of 71.

Charles Windolph left the army in 1883 and worked as a harness maker for the Homestake mines in the Black Hills. He died in 1950 at the age of 98.

Wooden Leg scouted for the army and became a tribal judge on the Northern Cheyenne Reservation in Montana. In the 1920s, he told his story to Dr. Thomas Marquis *(see Selected Sources).* Wooden Leg died in 1940 at the age of 82.

Young Hawk and eight other Arikara scouts told their stories to representatives of the North Dakota Historical Society in 1912 *(see Selected Sources).* He died four years later at age 56.

EDUCATIONAL EXTENSIONS

1. What is the "foreword" of a book? How does a book's foreword add meaning to the text? Read the foreword of *Remember Little Bighorn* and research its author, John A. Doerner. Why do you think he was chosen to write the foreword? What important background information did you gain about the topic?

2. Do you believe this event in history to be fact or fiction? Explain, and cite examples from the text.

3. How does the structure of the text contribute to the meaning and style? Describe the structure of *Remember Little Bighorn*, including its use of illustration, photography, sidebars, and text. Give examples of how the presentation of information enhanced your understanding of the content. Analyze the significance and importance of primary and secondary sources in this book.

4. How does an individual's personal experience enhance our understanding of history? Choose three personal accounts from the text and compare different perspectives on the war and happenings of the time. Distinguish between fact, opinion, and reasoned judgment. Analyze the relationship between primary and secondary sources.

5. Discuss Walker's characterizations of both George Armstrong Custer and the Lakota and Cheyenne. Find primary sources to support or refute his claims.

More to ponder ...

- Why do authors write nonfiction? How can reading nonfiction shape our ideas, values, beliefs, and behaviors?

- What can we learn from reading real-life accounts of history? How are you affected when reading different points of view? How do the histories of earlier groups and individuals influence later generations?

- How has the world changed from the time period of the text? How do you think it will change in the future?

- Research a topic from the book. Compare and contrast information and details that you found from different sources.